Acad

Lao-Tzu

Quotes... Vol.29

by The Secret Libraries

Paperback EDITION
Find us on:

The Secret Libraries

Published by The Secret Libraries for 2017
www.theSECRETlibraries.com

Paperback:
ISBN-13: 978-1973704249
ISBN-10: 1973704242

Quotes...

This book provides a selected collection of 193 quotes from the works of Lao-Tzu.

Lao-Tzu

6th–5th century BC

Do the difficult things while they are easy and do the great things while they are small. A journey of a thousand miles must begin with a single step.

When you are content to be simply yourself and don't compare or compete, everybody will respect you.

"

When I let go of what I am, I become what I might be.

"

The Way is empty, yet inexhaustible, like an abyss!

When wisdom and knowledge appear, great pretense arises.

Those who understand others are clever, those who understand themselves are wise.

What should be shrunken must first be stretched.

It (Tao) is eternally without desire. So, it can be called small. All things return to it, although it does not make itself their ruler. So, it can be called great.

"

What should be deprived must first be enriched.

"

Returning is the movement of the Way.

The superior student listens to the Way and follows it closely. The average student listens to the Way and follows some and some not. The lesser student listens to the Way and laughs out loud. If there were no laughter it would not be the Way.

The straightness of the Way seems curved.

When everyone in the world sees beauty, then ugly exists.

The whole world says that my Way is great like nothing else. It is great because it is like nothing else. If it were like everything else, it would long ago have become insignificant.

The nameless is the beginning of Heaven and Earth.
The named is the mother of all things.

From now back to antiquity, its (Tao's) name has not been lost. Thereby, see the origin of all.

The one who does not honor the teacher and the one who does not honor the task, although ever so knowledgeable, they are confused.

All things in the world are born out of being. Being is born out of non-being.

The world's beginning is its mother. To have found the mother is also to know the children. Although you know the children, cling to the mother. Until your last day you will not be harmed.

Can you make your soul embrace the One and not lose it?

“

The progress of the Way seems retreating.

”

Hold on to the ancient Way to master the present, and to learn the distant beginning.

Knowledge of the eternal is all-embracing. To be all-embracing leads to righteousness, which is majestic.

Those who are right do not argue. Those who argue are not right.

The greatest virtue is to follow the Way utterly.

The sage embraces the one, and is an example to the world.

Hold on to the great image, and the whole world follows, follows unharmed, content and completely at peace.

What is and what is not create each other.

Profound virtue is indeed deep and wide. It leads all things back to the great order.

High and low rest on each other.

Things exalted then decay. This is going against the Way. What goes against the Way meets an early end.

The great Way is very straight, but people prefer to deviate.

Heaven's Way does not contend, yet it certainly triumphs. It does not speak, yet it certainly answers. It does not summon, yet things come by themselves. It seems to be at rest, yet it certainly has a plan.

First and last follow each other.

True words seem false.

All things flourish, and each returns to its source.

Strong winds do not last all morning, hard rains do not last all day.

If Heaven and Earth are unable to persist, how could man?

True words are not pleasing. Pleasing words are not true.

What the Way is to the world, the stream is to the river and the sea.

"

What should be abolished must first be cherished.

"

A good person is the bad person's teacher. A bad person is the good person's task.

Of all things, none does not revere the Way and honor virtue. Reverence of the Way and honoring virtue were not demanded of them, but it is in their nature.

The river and the sea can be kings of a hundred valleys, because they lie below them.

"

Heavy is the root of light.

"

The world is a sacred vessel that cannot be changed. He who changes it will destroy it. He who seizes it will lose it.

Being a model to the world, eternal virtue will never falter in you, and you return to the boundless.

A good mooring needs no knot, still no one can untie it.

Conquering the world and changing it, I do not think it can succeed.

Those who are quiet value the words. When their task is completed, people will say: We did it ourselves.

When the uncarved wood is split, its parts are put to use. When the sage is put to use, he becomes the head.

If Heaven were not clear it might rend. If Earth were not firm it might crumble.

What has no substance can penetrate what has no opening.

The most complete seems lacking. Yet in use it is not exhausted.

When the great Tao is abandoned, benevolence and righteousness arise.

What's the difference between beautiful and ugly?

Those who know are not learned. Those who are learned do not know.

Who can wait in stillness while the mud settles?

A good traveler has no fixed plans, and is not intent on arriving.

Abandon wisdom, discard knowledge, and people will benefit a hundredfold.

Being deeply loved by someone gives you strength, while loving someone deeply gives you courage.

Truly, only those who see illness as illness can avoid illness.

A climb of eight hundred feet starts where the foot stands.

At the center of your being you have the answer; you know who you are and you know what you want.

What should be weakened must first be strengthened.

People starve. The rulers consume too much with their taxes. That is why people starve.

Mastering others is strength. Mastering yourself is true power.

There is no greater misfortune than greed.

"

Abandon knowledge and your worries are over.

"

"

I have the mind of a fool, understanding nothing.

"

All things carry yin and embrace yang. They reach harmony by blending with the vital breath.

When the palace is magnificent, the fields are filled with weeds, and the granaries are empty.

Behave simply and hold on to purity.

The most difficult in the world must be easy in its beginning.

"

Solve it before it happens. Order it before chaos emerges.

"

A multitude of words is tiresome, unlike remaining centered.

A tree as wide as a man's embrace grows from a tiny shoot.

Returning to the source is stillness. It is returning to one's fate. Returning to one's fate is eternal.

Letting the mind control the vital breath is called force.

Those who show no trust will not be trusted.

The valley spirit never dies. It is called the mystical female.

Those who seek knowledge, collect something every day. Those who seek the Way, let go of something every day.

> **Can you** open and close the gate of Heaven and act like a woman?

The highest tone is hard to hear.

"

There is no greater crime than desire.

"

Sometimes gain comes from losing, and sometimes loss comes from gaining.

All things arise in unison. Thereby we see their return.

The more clever and cunning people are, the stranger the events will be.

Words spoken about the Way have no taste. When looked at, there's not enough to see. When listened to, there's not enough to hear. When used, it is never exhausted.

There is no greater disaster than discontent.

People are difficult to rule, because of their knowledge.

A good door needs no lock, still it can't be opened.

Knowing honor, but clinging to disgrace, you become the valley of the world.

If the sage wants to stand above people, he must speak to them from below. If he wants to lead people, he must follow them from behind.

"

The light of the Way seems dim.

"

My words have an origin. My deeds have a sovereign. Truly, because people do not understand this, they do not understand me.

"

That so few understand me is why I am treasured.

"

Without desire there is stillness, and the world settles by itself.

Not praising the deserving prevents envy.

The highest virtue is not virtuous. Therefore it has virtue.
The lowest virtue holds on to virtue. Therefore it has no virtue.

Man is ruled by Earth. Earth is ruled by Heaven. Heaven is ruled by the Way. The Way is ruled by itself.

He (the Sage) does not show off, therefore he shines.

There was something that finished chaos, born before Heaven and Earth.

Thirty spokes are joined in the wheel's hub. The hole in the middle makes it useful.

Is not the space between Heaven and Earth like a bellows? It is empty, but lacks nothing. The more it moves, the more comes out of it.

Not knowing of the eternal leads to unfortunate errors.

Can you comprehend everything in the four directions and still do nothing?

To have enough of enough is always enough.

Those who know it do not speak about it. Those who speak about it do not know it.

Misery is what happiness rests upon. Happiness is what misery lurks beneath.

Correct becomes defect. Good becomes ominous. People's delusions have certainly lasted long.

Never take over the world to tamper with it. Those who want to tamper with it are not fit to take over the world.

Knowing that you do not know is the best. Not knowing that you do not know is an illness.

Pounding an edge to sharpness will not make it last.

Knowing the bright, but clinging to the dark, you become a model to the world.

Only I am clumsy, like drifting on the waves of the sea, without direction.

He who holds on to the Way seeks no excess. Since he lacks excess, he can grow old in no need to be renewed.

Filling all the way to the brim is not as good as halting in time.

"

The Way is ever without action, yet nothing is left undone.

"

The sage never strives for greatness, and can therefore accomplish greatness.

Lessen selfishness and restrain desires.

The value of teaching without words and accomplishing without action is understood by few in the world.

Free from desire you see the mystery. Full of desire you see the manifestations.

Use justice to rule a country. Use surprise to wage war. Use non-action to govern the world.

The sage honors his part of the settlement, but does not exact his due from others.

Those who have the courage to dare will perish. Those who have the courage not to dare will live.

Moderation means prevention. Prevention means achieving much virtue.

Kindness in words creates confidence. Kindness in thinking creates profoundness. Kindness in giving creates love.

The sage knows without traveling, perceives without looking, completes without acting.

Be content with what you have; rejoice in the way things are. When you realize there is nothing lacking, the whole world belongs to you.

> Obscure, like muddy waters.

The sage is sharp but does not cut, pointed but does not pierce, forthright but does not offend, bright but does not dazzle.

Nature does not hurry, yet everything is accomplished.

I do not act, and people become reformed by themselves.

Although he travels all day, the sage never loses sight of his luggage carts.

Cautious, like crossing a river in the winter.

Seal the openings, shut the doors, and until your last day you will not be exhausted. Widen the openings, interfere, and until your last day you will not be safe.

Those who act will fail. Those who seize will lose.

Ancient masters of excellence had a subtle essence, and a depth too profound to comprehend.

Lightly given promises must meet with little trust.

Fine words are traded. Noble deeds gain respect. But people who are not good, why abandon them?

If I have just an ounce of sense, I follow the great Way, and fear only to stray from it.

Praise leads to weakness. Getting it causes fear, losing it causes fear.

By compassion one can be brave.

I have three treasures that I cherish. The first is compassion. The second is moderation. The third is not claiming to be first in the world.

Why did the ancients praise the Way? Did they not say it was because you find what you seek and are saved from your wrongdoings?

When leading people and serving Heaven, nothing exceeds moderation.

I do not know its name. I call it the Way. For the lack of better words I call it great.

The sage regards things as difficult, and thereby avoids difficulty.

The sage knows himself, but does not parade. He cherishes himself, but does not praise himself.

People fail at the threshold of success. Be as cautious at the end as at the beginning. Then there will be no failure.

To be of few words is natural.

Seal the openings, shut the doors, dull the sharpness, untie the knots, dim the light, become one with the dust. This is called the profound union.

I have no desire to desire, and people become like the uncarved wood by themselves.

Keeping plenty of gold and jade in the palace makes no one able to defend it.

Those who know when they have enough are rich.

Displaying riches and titles with pride brings about one's downfall.

Abandon cleverness, discard profit, and thieves and robbers will disappear.

They can see their neighbors. Roosters and dogs can be heard from there. Still, they will age and die without visiting one another.

The sage puts himself last and becomes the first.

"

The highest benevolence acts without purpose.

"

Without stepping out the door, you can know the world.

The sage has no concern for himself, but makes the concerns of others his own.

Supreme good is like water. Water greatly benefits all things, without conflict. It flows through places that people loathe. Thereby it is close to the Way.

Those who stay where they are will endure.

The sage acts without taking credit. He accomplishes without dwelling on it. He does not want to display his worth.

Other people are joyous, like on the feast of the ox, like on the way up to the terrace in the spring. I alone am inert, giving no sign, like a newborn baby who has not learned to smile.

People turn their eyes and ears to him (the sage), and the sage cares for them like his own children.

See others as yourself. See families as your family. See towns as your town. See countries as your country. See worlds as your world.

Where there is no conflict, there is no fault.

Other people have more than they need, I alone seem wanting.

Peace and quiet govern the world.

Some have lavish garments, carry sharp swords, and feast on food and drink. They possess more than they can spend. This is called the vanity of robbers. It is certainly not the Way.

Those who are one with deprivation are deprived of deprivation.

Heaven's Way is like stretching a bow. The high is lowered and the low is raised. Excess is reduced and deficiency is replenished. Heaven's Way reduces excess and replenishes deficiency. People's Way is not so. They reduce the deficient and supply the excessive.

He (the sage) is good to those who are good. He is also good to those who are not good. That is the virtue of good.

The virtuous carry out the settlement, but those without virtue pursue their claims.

The sage does not hoard. The more he does for others, the more he has. The more he thereby gives to others, the ever more he gets.

The Way is the source of all things, good people's treasure and bad people's refuge.

In ancient times, those who followed the Way did not try to give people knowledge thereof, but kept them ignorant.

"

The noble must make humility his root.

"

A good wanderer leaves no trace.

Those who are one with deprivation are deprived of deprivation.

Cultivate virtue in yourself, and it will be true.

"

Must one dread what others dread?

"

When people are unsettled, loyal ministers arise.

Praise and disgrace cause fear.

The reason for great distress is the body. Without it, what distress could there be?

If people live in constant fear of death, and if breaking the law is punished by death, then who would dare?

When the Way is lost there is virtue. When virtue is lost there is benevolence. When benevolence is lost there is righteousness. When righteousness is lost there are rituals.

When much virtue is achieved, nothing is not overcome.

Rituals are the end of fidelity and honesty, and the beginning of confusion.

If people are not afraid of dying, why threaten them with death?

Lao-Tzu

6th–5th century BC

Free...

Receive a Kindle Edition in the series for FREE...

Sign up at

www.the**secret**libraries.com

Find us on:

The Secret Libraries

Published by The Secret Libraries for 2017
www.theSECRETlibraries.com

Paperback:
ISBN-13: 978-1973704249
ISBN-10: 1973704242

For more information please find us at:

www.theSecretlibraries.com

Thank you for your purchase.

11091619R00109

Printed in Great Britain
by Amazon